1985

THE NATIONAL POETRY SERIES, 1984

WILD

THE NATIONAL POETRY SERIES

ONION

POEMS BY

Robert L. Jones

Graywolf Press

ACKNOWLEDGMENTS

I would like to thank the editors of the following publications in which some of these poems first appeared: *Choice* (Chicago), *Eye Prayers*, *Hawaii Literary Review, Lotus, The Missouri Review, North American Review, Pacific Review, Ploughshares, Poetry Northwest, Poetry Now, Skywriting, The Southern Review, Sumac, Three Rivers Poetry Journal*, and *Tugboat*; also, *Down at the Santa Fe Depot: 20 Fresno Poets*, James Baloian and David Kherdian, Editors (Fresno, CA: Giligia Press, 1970), and *Just What the Country Needs, Another Poetry Anthology*, Dennis Saleh and James McMichael, Editors (Belmont, CA: Wadsworth Publishing Company, Inc., 1971).

Twelve of these poems were also previously published as a chapbook entitled *The Space I Occupy* (Kalamazoo, MI: Skywriting/Blue Mountain Press, 1977).

Thanks also to Richard Katrovas, and to Howard Norman for the wild onion.

Designed by Tree Swenson; Palatino type set by Walker & Swenson, Book Typographers; manufactured by Thomson-Shore.

Published by Graywolf Press
P.O. Box 142, Port Townsend, Washington 98368

For my mother
RACHEL VAUGHT JONES
and for my late father
HERBERT MANNING JONES

CONTENTS

I

From Him

From his face
we got the cloud that hung there
we got the weatherless days inside

From his fingers we got the upturned

From his forearms
we got the hairless part
raised up to protect

From his elbows we got
held off
we got angry and they softened

From his shoulders we got the bones
we got a ride on top
and a handful of cold scalp
before we got dropped

From his chest and back
we got a boulder to warm ourselves at

From his crotch we got just enough to get by

From his thighs we got led to his knees
where we got the black
of the rubbed oil of his palms

From his feet
we got the odor of constant repair

From his heart

From the cord in his backbone
we got just enough light
to see the dusty benches that line his heart

And from the scars on its walls
we got shadows
that fit like our own flesh

Our Hearts

Here is the heart that languishes
the heart grown conscious of itself
it puts itself to bed
and wakes to itself
shining in through the window

Here is the hardening heart
just home from the office
it is put to sleep between the shoes

Here too is the lady heart
left all night in the bathroom
among the stray hairs and lipsticks

There is the heart that succeeds the body
that lives on and on
swimming in a spoonful of gray blood

There is the heart
that was sealed from the beginning
in its own black bag

There the speaker of perfect English
with its lips of pink scar tissue

The heart in the pocket like change
The heart below
in place of the testicles

We have seen the heart on the side of the official car
and the empty breast on business

We have seen our own hearts
and they wouldn't speak to us

They sat back
they folded their four arms about themselves
and went to sleep in our shirts

A Border Rose

(Tijuana/San Ysidro, returning)

Four cars back from the checkpoint, Sunday
at dusk, and the radio and I are arm-
in-arm belting out "Guadalajara" when
a third voice, static-free and in tune,
joins us: it's the rose man!
We're the best mariachi trio ever!
We're so good the radios around us tune in
on their own, and the tourists, suddenly bi-lingual,
are with us, and the blanket seller, a family's worth
draping his shoulders, and the ceramics vendor,
one shoulder sustaining a flat-backed elephant,
the other a roped-together farrow of piglet-banks,
and the dead-battery man, parking for once
his live shopping-cart garage, with us too.
Even the border guard, who bends to one knee, arms outspread,
and croaks out the last few bars.
I'm about to spring from the car and hug them all
when I realize I'm next.
Instead I buy one white rose.
I pull up and the guard is all smiles,
his first since he took the job.
I tell him I'm a citizen
but my rose is alien and undocumented,
and he loves it, waving us through with both arms.
But ten miles toward home and ten to go,
I wonder how long it's been without water.
I turn on the interior light
and it's, no, not possible.
I pull over. But even flash-lit
it's pink.
Match-lit, moon-lit, streetlamp-lit,

it's still pink, and getting pinker and pinker
until it's red, then a red
so deep and real I'm a paramedic
flattened to the wall of the van,
afraid to touch the heart smoldering before me.
That's your rose.

for PATRICIA, *the Rose Woman*

Water

Water is given the germs of mineral and vitamin
and it comes to be blood,
comes to be milk and the sweet jelly for sperm,
and it finds its way out.

Water is given salt, given alcohol,
it is given a thousand particles of death each day,
and still it finds its way out.

II

It comes when I think I am most contained.
From the corner of my eye
and the eye of my cock,
from the tear in my thigh, from armpits,
fingertips and forehead,
water breaks out red, yellow, white,
no color at all.

The time will come when I am emptied of it,
when what I trust loves me
drowns me as it leaves, and there will be
a few inches of bark drying in the sun,
waiting for water to come down and dissolve it.

Fat

I

When she smiles,
if she's able after the endless meals,
bedclothes, floors,
after putting away her steaming crack-faced shoes,
the fat woman wants her child
to take hold of the physical smile,
to sink in its fingers.

The fat woman lifts her stiffened blouse,
and the child sucks,
watching the sway of the half-moons of fat
suspended between elbow and armpit,
as she pats its back;

and there it learns what graceful is.

II

I thought once that if I could see it raw,
a patch of arm-flesh peeled back,
I would find, in bone beneath the fat,
the desire for wing.

I see now it's the fat she needs most,
its slow flame keeping us –
propped on bones – living,
as she diminishes.

Insulted Spirits

A few men are plodding home;
their breath fogs,
kissing them awake the last long block.
Their lips, scraping, say nothing,
their eyes are pieces of gray snow,
their feet are disappearing.

They tilt into the wind, cupping
their insulted spirits in their overcoats
as though they'd stolen them.

They were the witnesses
of this day's birth,
celebrated by cigarettes that went out,
by drinks that spit their dregs
into sleeping teeth,
and now by these men stepping out
the length of their solitude.

They are the ones that crawled out
of last night's wound before it closed,
what the dawn bled
to make itself presentable.

Depression

for ELISE *and* PAULA

I want a depression who is cleaner-shaven, better-dressed,
and generally a better citizen than I.

A depression who bakes his own bread, grows his own bean
    sprouts,
and drinks the oldest Beaujolais from the oldest French village.

And when we've eaten and drunk together,
a depression who will tell me all about himself.

Relaxed finally, a mahogany toothpick in his fingers,
he will bare his teeth,
and I will see they are bad teeth.

I want a depression who is self-conscious.

One I can intimidate until his face shrivels
to a prune of self-doubt

and can embarrass to a giggle that makes people turn their backs
and walk quickly away.

On the other hand, I'd take a hard-core,
second-class depression looking for a new lease on life.

One I can hire right off the unemployment line.

Because if I can hire him, I can fire him.

I want a non-union depression.

I want a depression who failed his assignation.

The failure of the dentist with false teeth,
or the bald barber,
the dermatologist with psoriasis,
the lethargic anesthesiologist,

they are nothing beside the depression who is depressed.

The Stone House,
Emma Cobb, Mr. Gin and Me

to DAVID GRATH, *the Dwarf-King*

I

This is for Emma Cobb,
chiropractor,
assembler of this house.

Who "adjusted segments of the spinal column";
who carried stone after stone
until her spine readjusted itself
to the shape of a question her body would ask forever;
who then continued with cement;
who built a gazebo where she could sit through
late afternoon thunder showers.

* * *

The doors are skinny,
the windows I have to bend to,
cupboards one cup deep.
Your dwarfish nature is everywhere, Emma.
You stretched hot water pipes through the rooms
so they'd chuckle at your utterings.
Even the stones spoke to you,
thumping down drops to the oil room
when it rained.

I wish I knew what your life was like
in this house, which I love
and cannot live up to.
The words have faded from the notes
you filled the cracks with.

This must be your gravestone, Emma,
your second body.

14

This one's for a lonely man
who lived here once.

Who got up;
who left a plate half-full of food,
a pot of peas on the stove,
clothes in the closet, and empty gin fifths
bobbing up out of every drawer and closet
whose mystery he couldn't solve;
who just got up and drove off.

* * *

Mr. Gin,
either your own emptiness
loomed up from the Salisbury steak and peas
so suddenly
all you could do was step on the gas,

or you had a vision of where Emma was.
Maybe the moon, drunk,
reeled down and gave a slow wink
that said *Go find her.*

I wish I'd been the one to unlock the door
to a half-year's gin stink.
I'd have gone through your things,
I'd have found you and asked *What the hell was it
that drove you out?*

III

This one is for me.

Who assembles sentences;
who senses around every exposed pipe
and wrong angle the presence
of two lives he'd like to speak to;

who makes up characters from stories he's heard;
who speaks,
hoping the echo comes back different.

* * *

Emma, Mr. Gin,
if we three are to meet
it will be in this poem,
this scrawled-out diagram of a stone house
you're welcome back to.

Out of my solitude,
and my hundred-forty-five dollars a month,
I'm bringing you back.
Emma, you never figured what to do
with the upstairs door that opens to a long fall,
and Mr. Gin, you must be starving.

II

Annie

it fell to the women and children to keep
the walls of the public buildings clean of
the flesh and limbs of those hit in the bombing

The thin slap of a finger,
the uneven thud of a whole body, trailing
shoes, watch, rings:

you've heard them all,
and the outline of each as it hit
has its place in your heart

and your heart tells you that each
inhabits that same outline within the wall,
your wall

full of spirits and pieces of spirits.
Here is Philip's ear to whisper good morning to,
Nelly's right hand to shake as you begin.

Annie, each day your eyes burn shut
and you cut yourself,
scraping knuckles on knuckles,

and never complain, seeing that
though its surface grows more pocked
and its body fuller, the wall just takes it.

And when you leave the wall at night,
it is the leave-taking of two friends,
both knowing

that at the end of the war
you will take your place.
Whether in flight

or with a slight step up to miss the shrubs,
you will enter, be met,
and a great greeting will go up and float

along the wall as it enfolds you.

Setting This Down

There isn't a constellation out here
I could imagine as your face.
What I thought was a shoe announcing from the porch
was a black walnut thudding
to dissolve in the melting snow.
It's cold, and out here there's a vacuum
that wants me.

I'm setting this down for you, anyway.
Each sip of brandy sends up
a shower of light
to the black place in my brain
where you wait.
With each, an aura of your face.

But right now an aura isn't enough.
I think I breathed in a sliver
of that vacuum, the air so icy
I didn't feel it,
and now it's in my lungs and growing.

Tonight

Tonight you can't drown the bitterness
in your throat, can't
give it over to love or sleep.
Nor keep it from filling your hair and hands.
You sit with it on your own stone
at the shore of whatever benign liquid
laps at your feet.
You'd like to leave it there,
like a shell a hermit crab had abandoned.
But it's the crab itself,
needing a bigger prison with each escape.

Jenny at Eight

Her hearing burned shut by fever
when she was two,
my niece Jenny talks mostly with her hands.
Today when I interrupt her watering roses,
she's pressing muddied feet to the trunks,
eyes closed, soothing
the plants with her vowels.
I'm deaf to her languages, she remembers,
and smiling breaks off a rose and sweeps my mouth.
She watches me say "Thank you, Jenny,"
and her fingers begin to bend then straighten,
twist then point, as she pronounces vowels
I can't put consonants between.
Her smile dissolves before my moon-like face,
the fingers curl into their palms.
I understand nothing.
I am the enemy of communication.
I am the worm who ignores
all but the tunnel he's eating through life.
Jenny knows better, she
gives me the rose.
I eat a petal.
She watches, sucking a stem of grass.
I chew the rose stem, swallow its juice.
She watches, her fingers hugging, pulling for me.
I am the last hope she has for me.

Jeffrey

I

You figured the thumb to San Diego, a bus
to Mexicali, then that little bedroom you can write in
on the train to Mexico City.
And when you arrived we'd drink,
you, Linda, and I, the mezcal I'd saved
that tasted of tire-water but moved
the tongue to a language you'd love.
From Sonoma, just above the broken hip of California,
you'd sent poems that were
circus events on paper but deadly serious,
images colliding with others like electric cars,
the kids full of joyous shock
and warm spillable blood.

We waited.
Then Linda left, her guts invaded.
Finally I left too, sick of the shit job
and the solitude among millions, missing Linda.
I found classes to teach
and began waiting for you here.

II

Each of us had landed
in his corner: my house, Kalamazoo;
done with your poems, ours,
drunk or stoned, the after-class over.
We'd decided I'd die first, for the bad life,
then Michael for pure bad humor,
and next, David, electrocuted embracing his own guitar.
About you, the youngest, we couldn't decide.
Nine years ago.

III

I've just gotten home to this apartment, San Diego, from
which I strain to see the fear-whitened faces of the pilots
as they pass over so low, and always the whoosh of relief.
Linda calls, happy with her new place and with Joel. I
begin to read compositions. I have two hours before class.
I'm working well when your lady Michelle calls, hysterical.
I go to my class. I don't know what else to do. I give a class
on the composition of the poems of Jeffrey Miller and on
the tiny life I shared with him. That's what I'd thought to
do, driving blinded to school, but finally I give nothing. I
enter, smile (the muscles of my face berserk); I say *Read this*
and *Write that* and *For next week* and then no words come.
They stare. I say you died. And they, beautiful and humane
to the last one, each having already lost his Jeffrey, pack
up their books and leave me with mine.

IV

Damn you and your poems full of genius,
and goddamn the son-of-a-bitching lack there'll be of you both.
I can't undam the reservoir of feeling I have for you.
Damn you anyway, who avoided everybody's hug,
for shyness; you
who always sat behind me when I drove
so I had to shout to you,
cornered and comfortable.
Why back there, always, head tilted
to the glass, humming?
Why back there, then,
when the splintering glass crystallized both our lives,
mine still ignorant of yours ending,
and yours a red rain of glass,
drenching stop sign, dead shoe, this poem.

III

I Want to Lie Down

There is one woman whose voice
is the rustle of those long gold flowers
the moon lays down to bloom on the water all night.
It slips inside you
and goes on blooming, even though
you think your life is empty.

There is another woman whose hair
is one long reed
whose slide through your waters
draws you right out of your emptiness.

I don't deserve any of it.
Tonight I'm confused and sad
and I want to lie face down on the grass
for three hours.

My dog rolls onto her back and stares at me,
her eyes half-closed.
I'd have to stretch out on top of the gazebo
to be alone, where
the stars would peck at my shoulder bones
and the moon would dangle her stringy lights.

But from up there I'd see the faces
going out behind the fogged windows of the Northwest Unit
of the Kalamazoo State Hospital, where
the criminally insane pay with their lives
for their sadness.

The Space I Occupy

I

You lie in the arms of the snow
falling outside the window.
You looked out a long time,
then lay down.
I ask if you are cold.
You are.

Your body gives off the only light,
the bones
reflecting the bare bulb in the room of your life
whose door is locked.

* * *

You close your eyes,
you drift down.
Now there is clear water flowing between us.
Your legs are losing their edges,
your nipples open.

I want to be something one-celled,
dropped into the water above you.

II

Your cheeks draw up,
eyelids tighten,
then one jerked breath.
Without waking, you loosen your grip
on my hand, moan from far away.

Maybe you were looking for me
in the small space I occupy in your life,

and found me,
face-down in the snow.

Now you relax in your sleep,
almost smile.
There is a path you're following;
a fall afternoon, Michigan.
On it you see a blossom whose veins
have wandered to an image of my face.
You take it up and carry it with you,
like the Ojibwa girl
who keeps the wooden vial she cried into,
holding wild onion to her eye,
and now has the salt to remind her
there is always more than she can see.

III

I want to get up, get dressed,
get in the car and drive north on whatever road
allows me to think the least.
At dawn I'll stop and dig,
with the other animals, for onion.

I'm going to rub my whole body with it.
I want a sorrow that is pure,
that has nothing to do with people.

IV

You won't remember what you saw
in your dream.
The memory will float in your bloodstream
like a poem sent off
into the water by someone
so scared by what he felt
he won't show it to anyone but water.

31

At San Quintín

to L I N D A

The sea spoke to us,
coughing bubbles that burst on our feet.
It washed its vowels over and over,
not wanting to lie or mislead,
and left a chalk that spelled
nothing, that spelled
whatever it wanted to spell.

So it spelled
Go back, no one's to blame
and no one's not to blame, go home,
turn and walk in opposite directions,
one step for each year spent
breathing into one another, and turn
again and hug the space before you.
Then hug one another to the marrow,
it spelled, and then begin again.

Your Voice

We were sitting on the shore
of a party, watching the dancers' bodies
move in and out of their shadows.

The dawn arrived, exhausted
and bitten to blood by small mouths,
and with it your voice,
the voice of your girlhood wrapped in smoke.
You placed it in the pit of my stomach,
your goodbye like a boiled stone.

You are a welt in me,
a stone the river of blood flows over,
cools and polishes, turns
to a gem, edgeless and empty.

Three Poems after Yves Bonnefoy

I. MY EYES

They want you before them,
stripped of every defense.
They want to suck
from you the source of every gesture.

You won't deplete her, I tell them.
Then they present me with my own body,
the chest, for example,
with its semblance of a desert.

They point out how simple life is
in a desert.

I see her face illumined from behind the flesh
by a light
whose source is the source of every smile.
I am given the cold beauty of the bones.

Now comes the smile that creates its own mouth,
the final smile,
as the face divides
and her breath is freed and spread before me
and I walk through.

III. I ASCEND

I come to her in a place where night breaks
across her features
as though a black sun presided.
I kneel, and limb by limb
I ascend,
become whole again.
I take my place,
the reigning constellation in her sky.

First the hills and their few lifeless shrubs,
and now her body,
take on the stain of my hard starlight.

Dust

The light settles on your face,
white crumbs circling your mouth.
You sweep it
from the lapels and shoulder-straps of the dead
you're dreaming of.
You sweep it from the dress
you will marry in.

You are the smiling, beautiful corpse
that stands shrouded in dust
in the corner dreamt by him you'll wed.

Your breathing is the dusty wind of the plain
we saw, where the shrubs
exploded to their height for no one.
It is the wind that blows between us
as we lie here in different countries.

You could gather this dust, add water,
and make a loaf you'd die of,
and wake up smiling.

Let It Be Here

to LINDA *again*

Three o'clock entered you
like a lost nightmare come home in daylight,
like a swallowed yawn that rose
to be the cloud behind your eyes.
Every pore of you became a hatch
through which the air of three o'clock
passed freely.

Your mother poured down
four fingers of whiskey that day
to clean her weapon.
She breathed deep,
then exhaled the tiny knives
sharpened on your upturned throat.

You walked away;
your despair was so pure you became
the air that parted for you.
There was nothing left for her to stab
but the hole in her life shaped as you.

* * *

When you choose to come back to the physical world,
let it be here.
At first there's nothing through the snow;
then at a point in the air the flakes
fall more slowly and then don't fall
but gather and become your face coming toward me.

Something Else Begins

for JEAN

The tongue again slack behind the lips,
the nodding penis,
the fingers emptied of everything upon your body....

Each of the senses has groped
along the thread of its history and arrived
at this length of flesh which seeks
only itself
in something that is almost sleep.

Now the edge
extends itself, taking in
you, the bed, everything around me.
Now I rise to a room wholly my own,
lighted only
by the discarded selves
that have gone up in flame throughout the night.

I want to gather them up,
the glowing ones, and turn
to those two sleeping bodies so close to death,
to call them awake.

Good Night

In your eyes there's a stretch of white beach
growing whiter as you walk it, so white
the man who follows you must follow in the surf.
Above are gulls so white they can't scavenge
for dead things, so kind they won't fish for live,
and so they turn and turn until darkness.

In your daughter's eyes you and she
lie together on that beach, and if that man approaches
to touch you he'll be pecked to a fine white dust
by birds starved and bored as the dreamt sky
beneath which you are both safe.

Your eyes are the washed brown of the pier,
your daughter's black-brown, their whites blue.
I want to close mine and begin again,
like a salamander staring at the sun
until lids sprout, or don't.

                *   *   *

Close your eyes; try to sleep
When your breathing deepens, I'll go.
Outside I'll fling myself into the air
like a suit tossed off before jumping,
but defying gravity I'll rise
and go on rising until I can barely see you
when you leave for work. Unlocking your car,
you'll hear a gull's caw and look up,
remembering the beach: I'll be the one
whose face is averted.
The pain on your face that fears everything
will be unbearable to me.

Querido Roberto:

In the 4th floor of the Palacio Azteca hotel
I'll be waiting for you.
Look for the white satin gown, the red rose
between the middle and ring fingers of my left hand.
Look for the hair you untangled once
in the dark: it's brown, and tangled again.
My eyes are brown too
but you'll be looking for my mouth,
which you know best.
It'll be very red, more an unsucked candy
than the wound you imagine.

Look for them,
because Roberto, you'll never find me otherwise:
my flesh is the air I exhale.
You know I'm chalk-white in the dark,
but in light I'm nothing, I'm transparent.
I am more real when you dream me
than I am here, writing to you from Ensenada,
than I will be, seated before a white wall
on which only my gown will cast a shadow
when you come to see me.
Roberto, I don't know if I'm a body
just exploded into gas
or a gas cloud about to take form.

Do you want to love me?
Then love me, my astronomer.
I am the Milky Way whose milk is salty.

There's another man who loves me so hard I'm afraid
to kiss him.
He's dizzied by my whiteness,

my cumulus forehead, the stark red of my mouth.
Maybe you shouldn't come.
Maybe I love him.

No, please come.
Touch me anyplace uncovered.
I have to know if I can
be touched, my cells pressed and purpled,
or if I'm vapor dreamt up to make you
hurt yourselves.
September 6th from 8 on I'll be there.

Hasta entonces, Julieta.

IV

Afternoon

My mother's first breath was drawn
from the dry heart of afternoon,
and afternoon inhabits every house of her life.
Always the drawers and closets open
to its wooden spoons
and broken garments, its face smiling up
from scuffed shoes.
Always the afternoon is filled with the slow
procession through itself.
Always the air holds its memory,
carrying the odors of fifty years of food
and the grease that cooks it,
the odor of rust in the pits of her arms,
odor of her breasts' diminishing
and the blood that hardens within them.

This is afternoon that never gives way to stillness
when she most needs it to be still.
The half-formed gestures go off from her anyway;
they circle around her, describing the body of afternoon.
This is afternoon that never gives way to night
when she most needs to sleep.
It gives light to her small moons of breath
and to the daily scars of her ankles and hands,
the scar of her belly,
all shining like candles
for afternoon to find its way back.
This is afternoon that doesn't need morning.

It took my mother's place in the womb.
It has taken my place;
it entered, spread itself out,
and became the one moment worth two people's lives.

Our Last Visit

We sit facing for the last time,
a few feet apart,
the air quaking in our ears.
Finally the silence takes form,
an intimate presence
like another son who takes our hands
when we can't take each other's.

I see the essential face rise from you
a moment
in the failing light, Father,
its own light almost gone out,
so long neglected, so late in your life.

II

Now the night is complete.
It is beneath my clothes,
enters me,
and I am filled with its cold, black sky.

Is it the same with you, Father?
The same
that now clouds form
and a light snow begins to fall
through this night within me that promises to be long,
soft heaps of it
gathering on the sills of my ribs and hips.

Is it the same with you?
Your hair silver,
the stars of an inner midnight?

Grandfather Ashley, Back
from the Carlsbad State Sanatorium

It's August and the sun's bearing down.
Home is on its knees
beside the highway to San Angelo.

Behind the stuck yawn of windows
a few mesh ghosts
are waiting for some wind
to bring back their mystery.

Tumbleweeds huddle at the yard's rim,
the eyes of desert toads
staring out since Creation from their spiny circles.

Grandfather is back.
On the old Ford car seat outside the kitchen
he's watching a shadow drag
its weight across his khaki union suit.

Two Poems for My Uncle, the Barber

WILLIAM KENNETH VAUGHT (1919-1964)

One: An Atmosphere of Hair

I

There was an atmosphere of hair,
tiny filaments sifting through layers
of smoke, so the bars of light
the Venetian blinds shone down
were furred ropes I wouldn't pass through.

There were animals of hair
inching for my shoes
as his black Wellingtons
whispered semi-circles
around the 20th scalp of the day.
His scissors droned;
the backs of his hands bristled
with everyone else's hair.

When the strange necks had gone,
it was my skull
his slim fingers fluttered around.
Everything I was reached up
in chills to his clippers and crackling voice.

II

He came home one day
to his wife's heart thrashing
itself to mush, to its lying back
and the absurd whiteness of her face
that got whiter until it was chalk
that came off on his lips.

He went on barbering,
went on getting sailors past inspection,
skirting the caved-in middle,
until he went to Tijuana
and fell in
through the sunken middle of a $2 bed.

III

Something of him entered me
through my pores.
As his voice was wandering among his machines
looking for the metaphor
that would give his life to both of us,
his fingers eased the fear
from my neck, his palms
pushed their oils into my scalp.
Uncle to something that's dying in me
for never having been born.

Two: Before the Stone Settles Down for Good

You came to me one morning
after I'd walked myself
across the arc
between midnight and five
without falling into sleep or words,
after the pen dried up with waiting.

You came with the robins,
with the first sprays of light.
You came the instant after sleep
in a dream that hadn't had time
to draw up its plot.
In someone's black suit
you came with your baldness dulled,
your hands full of instruments.

All right.
The dead of San Diego wear their hair long.
One more, before
the stone settles down for good
on your forehead.
I'll go to sleep tonight
sitting up straight,
a whiskey in my fist.

I want to be drunk
when you run your trimmer up my neck,
so I'll hum off to sleep,
so my blood'll be thin
and the ropes running through it
that moor me to things
will dissolve
and I'll set out floating backward
in my bloodstream, singing
a celebration of baldness
and of nights that congeal around the waist
and rise like oil,
of whole lives that go down
like aspirin.

I float back past
the debris of marriages I watched
explode or just go slack,
past friends, scarred,
veered off into silence,
back through my brother's wordless
getting-up-and-going,
my father's presence like fog,
and into my mother's swallowed hysteria,
a tangle of free-floating, luminous roots:
she opens again, she pushes,
and I float back
through the day of my birth
and in among the still lilies,

the calm water
of my mother's life with you.

You are a being of memory –
scrubbed hands and cold clippers,
eyes that loved small things:
moles, creases of skin.
I want to trail my fingers over
your bald crown
to feel the blood rise to the surface cells.
I want to know where my blood came from.

How far back do you live, anyway?
In what remote cove
are you washing
the clipped hair from your socks?

Going Home at Night

I

It must be midnight, or later,
and the moon or a kind streetlight has sent
a few breaths of light through the drawn curtain.
I bend,
and I think I see the lines of her face deepen.
I see the part in her hair
which is the road I've taken, this life
its end.

The thing to do is place my mouth
at the dark palm
of the arm outstretched in sleep
and feed again.

II

Here is the emptiness, darkened,
and barely lighted by so early a dawn
the chill is from the inside.
It takes only a moment
for the smile to etch itself,
for things to settle out there around my shoes,
rising up like scuffed gravestones.

Now the hand whose life-line is so like my own
takes mine.
It leads me out and past my body,
into the world that inhabits hers.

Here is her brother, the barber,
looking up from a Tijuana hotel room,
up from a vision of his wife who was everything,

her heart burst on the kitchen floor,
her eyes still holding the dinner she'd made.
We see her death enter him,
fill his body like oil rising
until the light of his eyes flames up
an instant.
We see his hands changed,
the fingers now petals around two buds of air,
two flowers which bloom now
in another world.

Here is Mr. Ashley, the last
of the three husbands her mother outlived,
his face framed like a photograph in sepia
by the hard sanatorium pillow.
On the table beside him in his favorite room,
a saucer of cold coffee and his sweat-stiffened
union suit folded forever.

And her mother whose eyes are closed,
at peace,
whose back has grown straight,
whose hair is the color of earth again
and flesh again an orchard,
whose arms go off now
pulling her death along beneath the soil
to the dry edges of Texas.

III

The room is filling
with the dawn of the next day.
I watch the light give her features.
If she shivers
when she wakes,
it's because my whispers
have passed through an icy throat;
if she wakes
and asks nothing,

53

it's because her voice still
lies frozen
round the neck of a gravestone.

I have gone with her before.
I've seen the faces of her beloved dead,
looked into her face,
sleeping and awake, and I know
the dead don't talk to her.
They are busy being what they are.

It's she who wants to talk,
and I see now I've come home to listen.
She has just awakened,
warm enough,
and has asked me to make coffee.